ONE PAGAN'S

JOURNEY

ONE PAGAN'S
JOURNEY

VAJK FREYASMAN

authorHOUSE®

AuthorHouse™ LLC
1663 Liberty Drive
Bloomington, IN 47403
www.authorhouse.com
Phone: 1-800-839-8640

Published by AuthorHouse   10/23/2013

ISBN: 978-1-4918-2822-9 (sc)
ISBN: 978-1-4918-2830-4 (e)

Library of Congress Control Number: 2013918243

I would like to dedicate this book to my grandfather who was killed just before I was able to publish this book.

I love you papa, we will feast again together soon.

TABLE OF CONTENTS

INTRODUCTION

Have you ever wondered why a person would choose to be a Pagan or a Heathen? The very words Pagan and Heathen for most people today conjure up thoughts of people playing out medieval fantasies and crazy rituals. The fact is the Pagan community is full of some of the most humble and accepting people around. But what would make a person decide to take this path?

Since deciding to take this path I have found myself on many occasions having to explain to people why I chose to become a heathen. I found that I was able to express my situation and my beliefs better through poetry than I could in just regular conversation. I decided to write this book in hopes of giving some insight to others into why a person might choose this path for themselves. Contrary to popular belief, people don't choose this path because they find it difficult to abide by the standards of other religions. In fact in many cases the standards we hold ourselves to are more stringent than many of the other religions out there.

I hope that in reading these poems people can get some insight into why someone might take upon them this religion. I hope that even those that don't accept these beliefs can at least respect the decisions of others that have accepted them. I hope that those that may be thinking about this path can read these poems and realize that they are not alone.

No matter who you are, no matter to what religion you adhere, no matter your ethnic background, no matter your personal lifestyle, I thank you for taking the time to read my poems and listen to my thoughts.

May the Gods smile on you always!

Vajk Freyasman

A HAPPY YOUTH

Growing up Christian I was taught that if I did what was right I would receive God's blessings. I was assured by parents, Sunday school teachers, clergymen and others that God would provide for me and that great things lay ahead. This information provided me with a warm feeling inside knowing that no matter what happened things would work themselves out and I would come out on top. I learned that God loves each of us, and wants us to be happy and live up to our full potential. I recall many times when I attested to the fact that God had helped me or my family out of hard times. I believed these things without question as I grew to adulthood. Life was good.

A happy child with cares so few
Church and school the only two
School handled itself day by day
At the beginning and end of each day I'd pray

The Bible stories all I learned.
From Adams first breath, to the bush that burned
And comfort I felt as time went by
That I would be saved after I die

To church I'd go each Sunday morn
My Sunday best each week adorn
To listen to the teachers tales
Of Noah's Ark and Jonah's Whales

Vajk Freyasman

I learned that if I lived just right
And did my best with all my might
That I'd be blessed by God's good grace
And after death I'd have a place

But also I'd be blessed on earth
And receive according to my deed's worth
If I did what's right life would be good
And everything would be as it should

But if I did wrong
I'd feel God's sword
For "vengeance is mine"
Thus Saith the Lord

So, on I went through my childhood years
Bad grades and the Lord my biggest fears
And always the right thing tried to do
Mess up, repent, then start anew

I did the things just as they said
Morning and night I bowed my head
I knew that as I lived this way
I'd be watched over every day

That God knew what was best for me
Good fortune was my destiny
And while I did these things and more
I was sure to receive blessings galore

COGNITIVE DISSONANCE

As I got older and experienced new things, I noticed that the world around did not seem to match many of my religious beliefs. I started to realize that in my sheltered existence I hadn't noticed many of the inconsistencies that seemed to be present between what I believed and what I saw around me. (My existence was sheltered in part because I was surrounded by other Christians that all believed the same thing and in part because I was raised in the United States, a Country that is separated from most other countries by large oceans thereby protecting it from wars and other atrocities that plague many of the other countries around the world) As I traveled and saw some of the things that were going on outside my small bubble of a world and was later called up to go to the Iraq War, There were many things that I saw and was called upon to do that were in contradiction to everything I had believed up to that point. Many of the teachings of my religion stopped making sense and the explanations that I was given by clergy and friends made even less. It was at this point I began to feel that I could no longer accept what I thought I knew and this left me in a state of spiritual limbo. For many years to come I wouldn't know what to believe, only that I no longer believed what I had grown up with.

There I was, a married man
A child on the way and one in hand
Life was great or so I thought
But religion-wise I was distraught

Questions seemed to come to mind
Of the past and future of mankind
And when I made these questions known
Bible verses I was shown

Trust in the Lord, remember to pray
Fast and do righteous works each day
Serve your fellow man and kin
You'll receive your answers then

Love your neighbor
The golden rule
Read the scriptures
Stay in school

God works in mysterious ways
Or, that's what a man gets if he strays
No matter the question each answer the same
If you accepted them not you were supposed to feel
shame

As time went on I was called to War
Each Sunday I went to church just like before
Love all the earth's people the church leader said
Now let's figure out how to make certain ones dead

If God loves children as we know
Why did he allow that one child to go
Beneath that bridge where the land mine lay
That took his arms legs that day

I couldn't explain how years ago
God saved me from a deadly foe
When he gave me a feeling that danger was near
And thanks to him I was still here

Explain to the mother of that six year old there
That God loved me more or that's his cross to bear
Or maybe by chance if she would convert
God would help out and quell her heart's hurt

I'd drive by dead bodies lying next to the road
We couldn't pull over for fear they'd explode
So we left them right there, our safe shelter to seek
Then right back in church we would sit the next week

We'd sing and we'd pray and speak words of joy
Then back to the war fresh bombs to deploy
When asking the others why God lets this be
The answers would roll of their tongues gracefully

Man has his free will and God can't intervene
We must trust in the Lord for he sees what's unseen
For each person on earth, God has a plan
All we can do is the best that we can.

Vajk Freyasman

Still I wonder this day, if all have free will
Why then did he whisper to me on that hill
And warn me of dangers lurking about
Where's the free will of the man who stood
    there without
Who stabbed a young girl 16 times that day
Is my life worth more than hers, or that young boy
    at play?

Why then was I warned, but not that young kid?
My faith? My Righteousness? Good works that I did?
As struggled to deal with these spiritual strains
I developed a numbness that dulled all the pains
Strong feelings toward nothing I had anymore
And I moved on in blind faith as I had always before

I returned from the war to family strife
Things different between myself and my wife
The serenity I found in that numbness in war
Had spilled over into my marriage and more

I tried for a time to continue "Gods Will"
I prayed, and I read, served the church and yet still
I watched as my life seemed to crumble away
Financial woes, medical problems, marital dismay

Was this what the good Lord had planned for me?
My cross to bear? My destiny?
I thought faith and works would carry me through
That if I just knocked, God would answer me too

I did what he asked, where was my reward?
Instead of feeling blessed I felt more ignored
When a baby is born God gets credit and praise
Yet when lives are destroyed it's his "mysterious ways"

When bad things happen, it's a blessing disguised
And when this life is over we'll all be surprised
At the wonders awaiting for those that did right
So keep trudging in faith and sleep well at night

It seemed that my God was a big contradiction
He promised me hope that turned out to be fiction
As life continued to plummet straight down
My numbness became anger that I carried around

Anger at life but at God most of all
His will and his vengeance my soul did enthrall
None of his promised love did I see
Nor had life's experience showed there to be

So what does one do when his life passes by
And all the things he believed now seem a big lie
Does he just stop believing or does he find a new truth
One that brings joy like he felt in his youth

And so began my search to recapture that joy
That I distinctly remember I had as a boy
When my being was at peace both inside and out
But how would I get there, by what way, by what route?

OLD WAYS OF NEW

I was told by friends, family, and clergy that if I went through "the motions" in terms of religion that I would eventually come to the realization that it had all been true. But, the more I watched the events unfolding in my life and all around the world the more I began to believe that what I had believed in the past just didn't match what was going on. For a time, even though I played the role of a good Christian man, I considered myself to be agnostic and told myself "maybe there is and maybe there isn't a God". I went on like this for about 5 years when I started feeling guilty and hypocritical. I was teaching a Sunday school class and telling the students to believe things that I myself didn't, to do things that I myself had stopped doing. I decided that I needed to make a decision. Either I decide that there is no God and become an atheist, or I find a belief system that seemed to match the world as I saw it. I have a good friend that is atheist so I asked him some questions about his beliefs. I couldn't subscribe to the belief that when this life is over there is nothing beyond. Even though in my mind I felt that this might be the case, I really wanted to believe that there is more. So now I knew I couldn't be atheist, I couldn't be Christian, and I didn't like sitting on the fence. This left me with Islam, Judaism, or Paganism. (Pagan according to the dictionary is any religion that is not one of the "big three", Christianity, Judaism, or Islam.) Briefly looking at Judaism and Islam I could tell that both were still the one God controlling everything approach which I already knew I didn't believe. This left Paganism. The next decision was which pagan belief system to follow. The term Pagan, like the term Christian, covers a broad range of religions from Hinduism to Shinto, from Wicca to Heathenry. The concept of multiple Gods, the wills of whom sometimes may collide and cause chaos here on earth seemed more feasible than one God to me. When looking at all the different religions and groups of Gods I decided to look into my family roots. In 1907 the first of my family on my father's side arrived in the United States from Sweden. This means that my ancestors at one time believed in the ways of the Norsemen. For this reason I decided to look into Norse Polytheism.

A hole in my heart where my God used to be
No meaning to life no spirituality
I went through the motions, sang the same old song
But at the end of the day something felt wrong

Each Sunday in church I stood up and taught
And told kids to believe in the things I did not
This gave me deep down in my heart such a pain
Yet come the next Sunday I'd do it again

I went to the head of my church group one day
I told him my feelings, and that I just couldn't stay
He said the kids love you and enjoy what you teach
But I couldn't go on with no practice just preach

Vajk Freyasman

The time had now come to get off the fence
Was there a God? Was there not? a way that
    makes sense?
Perhaps there is more than one God up on high
Each acting his will as our lives pass on by

I concluded that there were more Gods than one
And each had a purpose and job to be done
To me for some reason this way seemed more true
But if this was the case, what was I to do

Which religions out there tell us there's more than one
And how do I choose where my future should run
Perhaps I should look at my family tree
If I lived years ago in what faith would I be?

The Swedes held beliefs in Odin and Thor
Freya, Frigg, Tyr, and quite a few more
Is this the path that I wanted to take?
I studied them more, a learned decision to make

Then there was the case of my family and friends
They would not understand how I came to these ends
Today's culture believes that these things are all myth
Like believing in Star Wars and Lords of the Sith

But how is that fair and why should this be
This faith was the norm before Christianity
The Christians came through the lands of the Norse
And made Pagans convert with harsh brutal force

A culture and heritage all laid to rest
Because someone decided that their way was best
So over the years forced conversions in herds
Soon Pagan and Heathen became dirty words

Those that held the old ways were treated like crooks
And their Gods today have become comic books
And the masses today can't see a good reason
Why someone would want to be Pagan or Heathen

I found this unfair and deep down inside
I picked up the Heathen banner with pride
The ways of the old would be my ways of new
Hail the Aesir, the Vanir, and the Folk Asatrú

FINDING FREYA

About a year after returning from a military tour in Afghanistan, my wife of 14 years asked for a divorce. This of course left me devastated for a time. I stayed up late at night worrying about what things would be like between me and my children. Would I still get to see them often? How would they handle the divorce? I would also worry about my future. Was I going to spend the rest of my life alone? I was 38 and this seemed a bit late to try and start over. My family and friends kept encouraging me to turn to God and he would help me through this rough time in my life. They didn't know that inside I had already decided to give up the religion that I had long since believed, nor did they know the religion that I had decided to take upon myself. However, they did have a point. If I didn't feel comfortable asking the God of my childhood for answers and comfort then I should ask the Gods of my current faith. I studied as best I could on the old ways and where my ancestors would have turned for guidance. As I read I felt a strong pull towards the Goddess Freya. Freya was not only a Goddess of war and a caretaker of soldiers, which I found appealing, but she was also the Goddess of love and beauty and was often sought out in matters of relationships. I knew that the primary form of communication with the Gods and Goddesses was through what was called a blót, where a drink was shared between Gods and Mortals. I decided to go on a search that day and find just the right cup to use for my first blót. I must have spent hours walking up and down the streets and shops of Monterey, California. I finally

found a goblet that seemed suitable and that night I had
my first experience with the Goddess Freya.

Marriage now over
Heart crushed on the floor
I'm 38 years old
Who'd want me anymore?

I felt life was over
Just go die in the woods
Nobody will want me
I'm all used up goods

My parents said pray and God will provide
Experience has shown that won't work, I have tried
Still nobody knows that my religion has changed
I'm not ready to tell lest they all think me strange

So alone in my room I'd sit and I'd stew
Starting over was not something I'd planned to do
But do something I must, can't just sit on the floor
So I grabbed my backpack and headed out the
    front door

Vajk Freyasman

If my old God won't help me, the new ones I'll try
So I read up on the ways of days gone by
Seems Freya was the Goddess they turned to in part
When it came to relationships and ways of the heart
And the way they would ask, back then they called blót
They'd have a drink with the Gods, that's what
    Sturluson wrote

I decided that I would hold blót on that night
But if I was to do this I'd do it up right
No ordinary cup would I use for this drink
Like an everyday glass used and thrown in the sink

So I walked into town, went from shop to shop
When I found the right cup I'd know when to stop
For hours I searched antique shops and more
But nothing seemed right till I spied on the floor
Of one antique shop where a goblet did sit
I thought to myself, that's the one, that is it

Goblet in hand and wine in my pack
A quick bottle of water and I started back
That night I walked down to a nice sandy beach
The ocean up to the full moon seemed to reach
I thought really hard on what words to say
I poured out a drink as was the old way

Freya, I said, as I held up the drink
I'm scared, and alone, I don't know what to think
Am I to be alone for the rest of my days?
My life is in shambles in so many ways

I sat and I pondered almost turning to tears
When I felt something inside I'd not felt now for years
Warmth from down deep seemed to stir in my soul
A feeling of joy, of regaining control

I smiled and I poured the wine onto the ground
Hail Freya, I said in a voice quite resound
Then poured I another drink into my cup
And with another "Hail Freya" I drank it all up

I put all my things back into my pack
And with a smile on my face once again headed back
Was this an answer that was relieving my stress?
It's up to the person that feels it I guess
For me I felt comfort I'd not felt in a while
Which was more than enough to warrant that smile

Since then I've had many more happenings like this
And I'm happy again in a spiritual bliss
And perhaps for these reasons I find it quite fitting
That goblet I used, on my altar is sitting

A FATED TRIP

So there I was, a new sense of spirituality that I hadn't felt in more than 10 years. I felt reborn and as I looked out over the world it was like I was seeing it for the first time. The grass seemed greener, the sky bluer, and I saw beauty in things that I had never noticed before. I could feel a happiness coming back into my very soul. There was also a connectedness that I began to feel with the world around me that I had never noticed before. I felt a deeper connection to my ancestry and those that had gone before me and truly wished that I could just sit down with them and chat about what things were like for them and how they used to handle situations. As time went on I felt the need to tell others how I felt. Not because I wanted them to do what I was doing or to agree with the path I had chosen, but because I didn't want to feel like I had to hide my new religion in order to avoid ridicule from friends and family. One Thanksgiving I was taking my children down to meet with my family in Texas and during that trip I had some experiences that pushed me to the point that I was ready to start sharing my feelings with others no matter the outcome.

It was Thanksgiving time one year
I was to take my children dear
To Texas to see family
An 18 hour drive 'twould be

I thought I'd start late in the day
The kids would sleep the night away
And I would drive in silent peace
Till morning when that calm would cease

As I drove south and the children slept
Frightening thoughts in my mind's eye crept
What if I was to fall asleep?
How would my children's safety keep?

What if a driver should come passing through
After having been drinking, his mind all askew
And with my car he did collide
With all my babies there inside

As I thought these things, I looked up in the air
And felt a feeling of comfort devoid of despair
When the full moon I saw sitting way high above
A symbol of Freya, her beauty, and love

I thought upon the Gods all night
And felt that I was in their sight
And they would keep a watchful eye
As we drove southward, my kids and I

A few hours later the sun came up
The moon not there when I looked up
It made me sad when I didn't see
That symbol of Freya looking down on me

And as I started to feel all alone
Two ravens I saw, cross the street they had flown
I smiled as I watched Odin's symbols fly by
And once again thought of the Gods up on high

Now sure there are those that will ask
    "what's so strange?"
The moon lights up each night and birds fly cross
    the range
But to me for some reason these sightings
    seemed more
I was noticing things that I wouldn't before

These things caused me to stop and give thought
To the way things all started and how far I'd got
That just months ago I sat on that beach
And the help of my Freya with life did beseech

And here was I now in a much better place
Warmth deep in my soul and a smile on my face
A girlfriend at home waiting for my return
Who showed total acceptance when my feelings
    did learn

I knew that there would be those that would scoff
Tell me Satan had stolen my heart and run off
Or perhaps they would laugh when they learned how I
    thought
Yet in others my beliefs could make them distraught

Or perhaps there are some that will make it a goal
To convince me I'm wrong and to save this poor soul
I hope that most see this for what it all is
I'm happy this way and it's none of their biz

Why would someone attempt to turn me from this
When it's made me so happy with spiritual bliss?
I like how I feel I don't want to go back
To the way things were then, with my life out of whack

When anger consumed me deep down inside
And I felt all alone no matter how hard I tried
No I think I will stay right here in my place
With the Gods in my heart and this smile on my face

I'm proud of my heritage, my religion, my choice
And I got a tattoo, a kind of visual voice
And although there are some that might think me a loon
Now gracing my back are Two Ravens one Moon

THE FOLK

After returning from my trip to Texas and solidifying in my mind the desire to practice my new religion in the open, I decided it was time to find other like minded people. I wasn't sure how to go about this. Most of the groups I was coming across were Wicca. Wicca, although a Pagan faith, is very different from Asatrú and Norse Polytheism. I decided to visit a couple of local shops in the area that cater to Pagan practitioners and came across a nice little shop downtown. When I walked in I met Dale and Steve. Steve is a Celtic Reconstructionist and Dale was an Asatrúar and regional representative of the faith. I told them that this was the path I had chosen and wanted to learn more. Dale would hold workshops occasionally in the back room of the shop to teach people about some of the traditions, or thew of the Asatrú religion. My girlfriend accompanied me to one of these workshops and we began to learn more about the religion and its beliefs.

Now that my mind was all resolved
I decided that I should get involved
With other people of Asatrú
Turned out tougher than I knew

Kindreds I looked for on the internet
I'm sure to find one there I bet
But as I looked there on the list
I found that many no longer exist

I continued to practice, all by myself
My make shift altar, one single shelf
I did my best with the books that I had
And now and then change my thew just a tad

My girlfriend would often join in with me
Whether it blót or conversation be
And although this religion wasn't quite hers
She supported me in both her deeds and her words

I did the best there on my own
But more I wanted to be shown
So once again took up the search
To find a Kindred, sort of an "Asatrú Church"

Hadn't had much luck online thus far
So I decided to jump into the car
To check out the shops there locally
To see where Asatrúars might be

Vajk Freyasman

We went from little shop to shop
And soon we thought we might just stop
One more was listed on the sheet
Off the beaten path, on a tiny street

We will check this one last place I guess
And If nothing turns up we will take a rest
So off we drove to find one more
Parked and walked into the store

Two men were standing just inside
I walked right up with a confident stride
I asked if they knew of Asatrú
I'd like to know more about the lore and thew

The men said yes and at a small table we sat
I told them my story, we had a nice chat
We talked about thew, the runes, and the lore
They showed us an altar in the back of the store

It was nice to know that it wasn't just me
There were others around that believed this to be
A couple weeks later we came back for a class
Where they taught more of thew and the ways
    of the past

They invited us camping, to meet with their kin
So we met on midsummer, and our hearts they did win
What a great group of people, so proud and so humble
I even teared up that night at the sumbel

We hailed the Gods, the Aesir and Vanir
The Ancestors, wights, the Alfar and Disir
The evening went on with laughter and toasting
And Just like the old days there was bragging and
    boasting

Midsummer now over, oh how time had flown
I'll forever be grateful of the great time they'd shown
We still try to meet at the turn of the seasons
Little coffee meetings and various reasons

I keep in my heart the great time that we had
The things that were said both the funny and sad
The feelings that deep down inside did evoke
Can't wait till the next time, Hail the Gods,
    Hail the Folk!

SO MUCH TO LEARN

Now that I had found others that felt the way that I did, it was time to focus my attentions on learning about the Gods and the lore. Unfortunately, the writings we have today are merely a fraction of what my ancestors believed. Much of the lore and the thew were passed on by word of mouth from generation to generation. It wasn't written down till years after the entire culture had begun to crumble under the Christian hoards. But I learned what I could and still to this day have much to learn.

The Clans and Kindreds now were found
Yet thirst for knowledge did still abound
My knowledge of Gods and lore still lacking
There was much to know, so I had to get cracking

The best place to start climbing this mighty hill
Was a giant ash tree by the name Yggdrasill
The tree that connected the nine worlds of old
The inhabitants of which all the stories are told

Asgard, was the Aesir's home
A glorious world where the war Gods would roam
And also there was Vanaheim
Where the fertility Gods did reign sublime

From Jotunheim the Jotuns Sprung
Jotun means giant in the ancient tongue
And Alfheim was the land of elves
Who mostly just kept to themselves

The dwarves all lived in Svartalfheim
And Forged things for the Gods from time to time
While Muspelheim, the realm of fires
Strikes Niflheim's Ice and creation inspires

There also was the land of Hel
For those who during peace time fell
The early Christians stole her name
And used it for their realm of shame

But to the norse Helheim wasn't bad
Just the land of the dead not a place to be sad
And last not least the world of men
Or Midgard as they said back then

Worlds all covered, now Gods to learn
And with each one their job in turn
Two tribes of Gods the Aesir and Vanir
Altogether too many to mention all here

There was Odin and brothers Villi and Vé
Who in the creation important roles play
Odin was to all the Gods king
He was the all-father and of him they'd sing
How his ravens, through the nine worlds would fly
And to obtain wisdom he gave up an eye

Vajk Freyasman

He hung on lifes tree to give us the runes
Not just a war God, but one of poems and tunes
Much was said of Gungnir his special spear
And his eight legged horse the mighty Sleipnir

Valhalla was Odin's drinking Hall
The Valkaries took warriors there after they'd fall
But only the bravest and best of the battle
At Ragnaroks coming would their swords and
      shields rattle

Odin's wife Frigg was Hearth's Goddess we're told
The Mother Goddess and ruler of the household
She knows what things in the future abide
But tells it to no one, and keeps it inside

The lore says that Frigg had many a handmaiden
Each one also with a special power was laden
Like Eir who was gifted the power of healing
And Fulla the Goddess of secrets unrevealing
So many handmaidens stood beside our dear Frigg
I can't mention them all lest this poem get too big

For sure anyone who has heard of the lore
Has heard the tales of the mighty thunder God Thor
With his Red Hair a blazing and Hammer in hand
He'd fight off the Jotuns and protect Gods and Man

Thor's wife was Sif with hair gold like the wheat
She was Goddess of the Fields and the Crops folks
      would eat
Loki, the mischief God, once cut off her hair
This caused the God Thor a great deal of despair

And just before Thor's hammer was Loki's demise
He's ordered to replace the hair highly prized
Loki goes to the world of the dwarves we are told
And there they spin Sif new hair of fine gold

We now come to Týr God of War and the skies
Who hand to hand combat Midgard's mortals apprised
Why then did he have only one hand you ask?
In front of all the Gods he did a very brave task

The mighty wolf Fenrir, Loki's son we have found
Had grown far too strong and had to be bound
Chain after chain strong Fenrir would break
Till the magical Gleipnir the God's bid the dwarves
    make

Fenrir, who sensed that his luck could go south
Insisted a God put their hand in his mouth
Týr was the god who accepted this end
When Fenrir couldn't break free, Týr's hand he
    did rend

Baldr was the son of Odin and Frigg
Innocence, peace and light were his gig
A God of Summer to mankind
Had a twin brother named Hod, who was born blind

It was foretold that Baldr would die
So Frigg went to all things on earth to try
To convince them not to harm her son
They all agreed to this, all save but one

Vajk Freyasman

The mistletoe made no such vow
But no concern, that could harm him how?
So all the Gods joined in a playful jest
And threw things at Baldr to give it a test

No matter what the Gods did use
It gave fair baldr nay a bruise
The trickster God, Loki, came passing by
He asked of Hod why he didn't try

Loki fastened an arrow of mistletoe
Helped Hod to aim and let it go
The arrow killed poor Baldr dead
And off to Helheim he was led

Váli, the God of revenge
His step brother's life did fast avenge
He killed poor Hod right then and there
The other Gods all looked on in despair

At the loss of Baldr the heavens cried
Nanna his wife of sadness died
The death of Baldr plagued dear Frigg
She had to do something, something big

The Goddess Hel, also Loki's child
Was sent word by Frigg how her son was defiled
She asked if Hel might Baldr send
Back up to Asgard, his death to mend

Loki told Hel to only allow
If everything on earth would make the vow
To cry over poor Baldr's fate
Only then would Hel send him back through the gate

So Frigg traveled the earth to make these things known
Loki disguised himself as a bitter old crone
And of all the creatures living here
It was Loki alone that shed not one tear

Next is Heimdal the guardian God
He decided who on bifrost would trod
From miles away he could hear the grass grow
And if there was danger a mighty horn he would blow

Bragi was married to the Goddess Idunn
On his harp he could play a lively tune
While Idunn tended to the tree
That grew apples of youth and vitality

These apples kept the Gods all young
And weren't allowed to just anyone
But Loki once stole them away
And gave them to the Giant Thiazi they say

The Gods without them began to age
And at the trickster God enrage
They forced Loki to steal them back
And kill Thiazi in a fiery attack

Thiazi had a daughter, her name was Skadi
And with her battle gear strapped to her body
She marched right up to Asgards wall
Vengence to seek on Asgardians all

The Gods were able to cool her head
And allowed her to choose from among them to wed
And in Asgard she would have a seat
But the groom she must choose by viewing only
    his feet

The eligible bachelors then laid on the floor
Showed their feet to Skadi, and nothing more
Skadi picked the finest pair
Found Njord, the sea God, standing there

Freyr, Njord's son, did one day sneak
And sat on Odin's throne on a mountain's high peak
From there he spied a Giantess
He fell in love and became quite a mess

He sent his servant to woo young Gerd
And couldn't eat or sleep till he heard word
The servant told Gerd he would take her life
If she would not be Freyr's wife

The Goddess Freya holds a special place in my heart
For it was with her my whole journey did start
Freya, the goddess of beauty and love
Had her drinking hall Sessrumnir in Asgard above

Not just a Goddess of love but a Goddess of war
She would ride into battle on a great battle boar
At the end of the battle when brave men would fall
The Valkaries would take some of them to her hall

Yes, Half the bravest warriors would quench
    their thirst
In Freya's Hall, and Freya got to choose first
Around her neck hung brisingamen bright
She had a cloak of feathers that let her take flight

Adored by the Gods, the Giants, and Men
But the God Od, her heart he did win
Od would go on journeys sometimes for years
And Freya would cry amber and golden tears

So there's a little of the lore
Believe you me, there's a whole lot more
And from them all great lessons learn
A place in Asgards Halls to earn

THE ANCESTORS

Respecting and honoring those that have gone before us was an integral part of this, my ancestral religion. This is actually a very common aspect of many of the pagan faiths. In Shinto and Hinduism there are at times entire shrines set aside just for the respect of your ancestral lineage. I have seen people attempt to connect to their ancestors in many ways. Some people may do it by playing an instrument that was common in times past that may not be common today. Others may do it by learning a trade that their ancestors may have held important such as brewing wine or forging metal. In any case an important part of Asatrú is respecting and honoring those that have gone before and living up to what has become known as the nine noble virtues so as not to bring shame upon your ancestors or your own good name. My collection of poems would not be complete if I did not include one about the ancestors.

I gaze across the landscape of this gorgeous
    country vast
And can't help but stop and think about
    my ancestral past
The way they lived their lives back then without our
    modern things
No microwaves or mobile phones or planes
    with giant wings

Back then they lived so differently, much harder
    than you and I
If we had to live our lives that way most men would
    break and cry
But they would go on day by day not shedding any tears
No, happy they would live their lives back then in
    ancient years

I think about a family gathered round a hearth ablaze
The smell of meat was in the air, a horn of ale they'd
    raise
They too would toast their ancestors and those that
    went before
And tell stories to their children of the Gods and
    raging war

Children all learned how to hunt and how to win a fight
How to find something to eat and then keep warm
    at night
I wonder of us here today, how many would survive
A full winter in the mountains, with just our wits to stay alive

I thank the Gods that war today is not as it was then,
Each man upon the field must have had the bravery
of ten
Face to face they would fight with axes, hammers,
swords
The wounded shrieking out in pain, blood running down
the fjords

Each man fought hard with bravery, hoping he would be
the choice
Of the Valkaries that would soon come down to charm
them with their voice
And those that survived the battle, then had to board a
ship
For the long sea journey to go back home and tell folks
of the trip

The family still back at their home waiting for their return
Carrying out the daily tasks their minds filled with
concern
Today we have telephones and emails we can send
To keep the loved ones notified, some happiness to lend

I think of a father and young son hunting in the woods
The family relied quite heavily for them to bring back
goods
It's not like when we hunt today and fail to make a catch
Where you can shrug it off, go hit a bar, and watch a
boxing match

Back then if you did not come back with venison in tow
Your family then would go without, a hard winter
to know
Could we have done it way back then without life's
luxuries
Indoor plumbing, mobile phones, cars, HDTVs

But then there is the other side, the simpler side to see
They wouldn't all just sit inside, gathered round a large
TV
Instead they'd sit around the hearth, the fire dancing
bright
Spend time together as a family, talk throughout
the night

The family bond was strong back then and bonds of
tribes were too
You had to stick close to each other, your part always to
do
There was a set of moral codes by which the folk abide
And those that could not keep them would be cast to the
outside

COURAGE you should always show when going
through your life
Whether this was on a battlefield or common daily strife
Standing up for your beliefs, and what you feel is right
Regardless of the consequence live by your bravery's
might

SPEAK THE TRUTH in all your dealings with both Gods
and man
A promise made should not be broken, lest dishonored
be your clan
As was back then your word today is what sets you
apart
Can you be trusted or can you not, on which side is your
heart

HONOR was a crucial piece of life in times back then
You strived to win the honor of the Gods as well as men
If your deeds bring shame upon yourself, your family,
your kin
How then the favor of the Gods did you expect to win?

LOYALTY to kindred, clan, your children and your spouse
Stand beside them come what may, protect them and
their house
A house, not just a building, made up of dirt and wood
But for all those living there inside it's also understood

SELF DISCIPLINE must always have, deliberate each deed
Don't let your actions be controlled like the river controls
the reed
Stand strong when you are tempted, to just go with the
flow
For the treasures on the other side are more than you
can know

When a wanderer comes to your door for food or place
　　to sleep
Don't turn them out into the night to like they were a
　　barnyard sheep
Do not forget the Gods at times roam earth disguised as
　　man
Until the wanderer is proven a foe, **YOU SHOULD HELP
THEM IF YOU CAN**

Do not rely on others, more than you do yourself
SELF RELIANCE is key, you alone should strive to stock
　　your shelf
In this way you will be prepared for the winter dark
　　and cold
Being able to do the job yourself is worth its weight
　　in gold

TRY NOT TO BE COMPLACENT with the way that
　　things are now
If something can be better, get to work and find out how
This can be an outer thing like your home in which
　　you live
Or an inner thing like eating right or how much love
　　you give

And finally, there is **PERSEVERE** no matter what weave
　　the Norns
Take what fate has thrown your way, then fill your
　　drinking horns
And say, "this will not defeat me nor will I let it hold me
　　back"
And if by chance it knocks you down, stand up, get back
　　on track

These noble virtues numbering nine were used back in
the day
To keep your words, your deeds, your thoughts all
heading the right way
And those that held these values high honored family
and kin
And the honor of the Gods themselves they were for
sure to win

We live lives differently today than way back at the start
But we should always keep our ancestral ways deep
inside our heart
Aspire to uphold these virtues that our ancestors put in
place
To honor them by living right, and win from them good
grace

MY ALTAR

When I first began to practice Asatrú I set aside a shelf
in my home to place things of importance. These items
reminded me of my heritage, my ancestors, and the
Gods. I had candles that I would light to honor them
and would reflect on my life as I watched the tiny flames
dance. Over time I have added things to my altar.
Some things I added because they caused me to think
about specific experiences that I have had other things
because they were gifts from Kinsmen and friends and
I felt that they deserved a place there. I am sure that
as the years go on my altar will continue to grow. For
now, this is a poem about the things that currently reside
there.

I had a make shift altar that I built back at the start
A few important items to show the Gods my heart
They all fit on a single shelf 6 inches by 2 feet
But as my journey did go on I found it incomplete

So one by one I added things as time did travel on
Items that reminded me of Gods or ancestors gone
Each Item held a special thought or special memory
So when I look upon them now it all comes back to me

The way I felt, the way I was, the way that I am now
Each time I stand before it I can reaffirm my vow
To keep the Gods and Ancestors a part of me each day
Live life with honor to be remembered after I have gone
     away

My single shelf has two become and now a table too
I stand before it every day and carry out my thew
The top shelf I give to the Gods, the Aesir and Vanir
The second shelf is for the wights, the Alfar, and Disir

The table is for items of my journey and my kin
And for Special Gods and Goddesses whose hearts I
     hope to win
Each Item sitting in its place awaiting my return
To stand before it once again the candles for to burn

The top shelf holds a drinking horn to give the Gods
     a drink
Beside it are two candles red, for when of the Gods
     I think
Above it hangs a knife and sheath to remind me of
     the days
When men would use their bravest deeds to show the
     Gods their praise

The second shelf a fountain holds to remind me of
     the earth
The land wights, and the seasons, and to all things
     a rebirth
The fountain holds two candles white upon the
     fountain floor
I light these for my ancestors and those that went before

To the fountain's left a dragon sits to remind me of life's
    tree
And how the mighty Nidhog gnaws its roots, or in
    essence me
And how I should withstand the pains and toils while in
    this world
Accept my fate no matter what the Norns for me unfurled

And on the right another horn that I made for myself
I use it when I toast the Gods then replace it on the shelf
A necklace with an onyx horn sits on the shelf as well
I wore this as my secret pledge before others I did tell

The table holds a knife to the left and a hammer on
    the right
Weaponry used by men and Gods whenever they
    would fight
Between them both are statues of the Gods that led
    me here
One for Odin, the all-father, and one for Freya dear

Before them each a candle sits so that I may honor
    show
And live my life in such a way that their blessings I may
    know
Also on the table a small bag with runes inside
To help unravel life's mysteries when fates of men
    collide

An offering bowl is placed as well for when I
    offerings make
To the Gods or to the ancestors for them to symbolically
    take
And next to that my goblet which for my first blót I used
And since that night on that sandy beach have gotten
    more enthused

Around the tables edges are gifts to me from kin
Pendants of Thor's hammer and a bag with herbs within
As time goes on I will add more and watch my altar grow
I wonder what it might look like in another ten years
    or so

I'm sure to have experiences, and make more memories
And I suspect that I will add a great deal more to these
And as I stand before it, in practice of my thew
A life of honor, bravery, and perseverance will pursue

RESPECT

At first glance the tendency for most people seems to be to dismiss Pagan faiths as silly or fictional. They will equate it to fantasy novels and movies and disregard many of the stories as simply unbelievable. But when you look at all religions on the earth, all of them contain beliefs that when looked at objectively, any person would find them fantastical or hard to believe. It all boils down to what a person believes is true or false. When you put any two faiths next to each other you will find a myriad of differences but also in most cases there are a great many similarities as well. This poem is in no way meant to mock any religion but simply to point out that all religions contain some of these fantastical occurrences in their teachings. What one chooses to believe over another is a matter of personal preference. In my opinion what one chooses to believe is a very personal matter and isn't something that needs to be debated.

When looking at the religions all around the earth
Each person decides for themselves each religion's
    worth
Then the people come together, oft in heated debate
Results are many feelings hurt, and in some cases hate

Fact is that all religions, if folks will simply see
Contain things that to others cannot possibly be
From a world that's created in only 6 days
To a being that can keep the whole Earth in his gaze

There is walking on water, turning water to blood
Talking snakes, talking donkeys, an entire Earth flood
People turning to salt or floating in air
A man with super strength if you don't cut his hair

When children made fun of a bald headed dude
He put on them a curse, and they soon were bear food
The entire Earth's population began with just two
A boat with more animals than the San Diego zoo

Thor's mighty strength people think it as odd
But Samson's great power, well that was gifted by God?
After this life is over up in heaven you'll walk
But if you call it Valhalla, well that's just crazy talk

Fact is that there are also many similarities
The Christians and Heathens both have special trees
That bore fruit that is meant for God and not man
With powers like knowledge or an eternal life span

In the Garden of Eden the bible says was a tree
Adam and Eve are ordered to leave the fruit be
While in Idunn's Garden is a tree of apples like gold
And they are the reason the Gods never grow old

What makes one tree truth and the other one not
One might tell you they prayed and an answer they got
But the other man is likely to say the same thing
Both believe they are right and the same song they sing

A priest in a church before an altar he stands
Consecrates water or wine which to the people then
    hands
I've learned that heathens do a similar one
But for some reason of ours people want to make fun

The Jews and the Muslims both think they're correct
The Christians think they're right and dismiss others as
    sect
A Buddhist will tell you he's in the right throng
While the pagan believes that all four have it wrong

This poem I write is not meant to poke fun
Or to say someone's wrong or that I'm the right one
It's simply to say all religions cast doubt
On the man standing there looking in from without

Remember next time you call a story a myth
That's somebody's faith that you're dealing with
Each person decides what to them is correct
Let's allow them that privilege, and treat all with respect

A NAME

In today's day and age you can find just about anything on the internet, including facts and information about just about anybody. I did a simple google search for my name and found a listing of past addresses, friends, and family. Unfortunately there are many people out there that if they happen to read my writings will become angry and decide that they must lash out at me. I accept that fact. However, I do not want them to attack my loved ones. These are my thoughts and my decisions and should not be used by others to cause my family pain or stress. For this reason I have decided to use a pen name when publishing this book. Below you will find a poem about the name that I chose. And to any and all that read my poetry may the Gods smile upon you!

No matter what my words may ask
I know some will take up the task
To mend the "errors" of my ways
Show me their hatred not their praise

And as I think about their hate
I don't want it to harm the fate
Of my children family and friends
For this reason I've come to the ends

That I must use a different name
To protect my kids, not out of shame
By which to publish my written work
And protect them from a would be jerk

This being said, what name to use
Where do I look, how do I choose
As through life's memories I lurk
I found two names that seem to work

I spent some time in Hungary
And while there studied their history
At one point they were Pagans too
Before Christian's came rolling through

King Géza was a Pagan King
Convert or die he heard them sing
To save his countrymen, this he said
"We will convert, lest we all be dead"

This left the country split in twain
Half wanted Pagan to remain
In civil war the country raged
And by that time Géza was well aged

He died before conversions end
Two men did for the throne contend
By Christian law his son was king
But they weren't yet Christian, was the thing

Vajk Freyasman

By Pagan law Kopány should rule
And so raged on this deadly duel
Until Kopány was one day killed
The Christian masses were all thrilled

The birth name of Géza's son was Vajk
This name the Christian's did not like
So Stephen then became his name
To rid him of his "Pagan Shame"

So I have decided that in this way
I'll revive the name they threw away
The first name Vajk will be my choice
When sounding out my Pagan voice

Now what should my last name then be
When looking back through history
In the northern lands there was a trend
That showed you how your name should end

If your father's name back then was John
You simply tack the word "son" on
So when the son of Olaf's life begun
The name he got was Olafsson

Others, to give the Gods due praise
Upon them a God's name would raise
So to their families, kin, and clan
Became Thorsson or Odinsman

Looking back to the night on that sandy beach
For the help of a Goddess I did reach
Since my pagan life with her began
I shall take the name of Freyasman

So Vajk Freyasman is the name I took
And to all those that might read this book
I hope that it makes to you known
That if you feel as I do you aren't alone

And to those that still must share their rage
One more thing I put on this page
Don't harass my kids, my dad, or mom
Come to me, vajkfreyasman@gmail.com

PICTURES

This is the goblet I used for my first blót in Monterey, California. It still sits on my altar today to remind me of that night and where this part of my journey began.

About 2 years after my first blót I had the opportunity to visit that beach again. I was very grateful for the comfort that I had felt over the past two years and wanted to return and thank Freya for that night. My girlfriend could not accompany me but sent a necklace for me to offer Freya by throwing it into the ocean. I too had a necklace to offer. That night I sat on the beach where it all began and thanked the Gods for getting me through a tough time in my life. I also thanked Freya both on my behalf and on the behalf of my girlfriend for us having found each other.

This is my altar as it looks today. I look forward to watching it grow as I add things that remind me of the Gods, Goddesses, Ancestors, and experiences that I will have.